KU-162-633

Is my cat a genius?

Is my cat a genius?

An exclusive edition for

This third edition published in Great Britain in 2021 by
Allsorted Ltd, Watford, Herts, UK WD19 4BG

Author: Helen Redding

Images used under license from Shutterstock.com

Cover design: Milestone Creative

Contents design: Jo Ross, Double Fish Design Ltd

ISBN: 978-1-912295-16-6

Printed in China

10 9 8 7 6 5 4 3

Cats are a mysterious kind of folk. There is more passing in their minds than we are aware of.

SIR WALTER SCOTT

Contents

If cats could talk, they wouldn't.

NAN PORTER

Introduction

If you own a cat, you'll know that it's impossible to just 'have' a cat. It becomes a love, an obsession, and friends and family will start to buy you cat-related gifts. Before you know it, you're a 'mad cat person', no longer a cat owner but ruled by your cat. How do they turn the tables on us like that? Looking into their eyes, you can see the cogs turning and can only assume that genius is at work.

But how do you know if your cat really is a genius? In this book, you'll discover how their brains work and gain an invaluable insight into their behaviour. When you understand what your cat's brain is capable of, some of their peculiarities might even become clear! Like humans, your cat might be clever at one thing and not another, they don't have to be an all-rounder to be amazing.

It's important to remember that even if your cat doesn't turn out to be a danger to Einstein or the other great geniuses of our time, they're still wonderful, funny, lovable creatures. Who needs a cat who can do algebra when you've got one you can share delicious cuddles with?

I have studied many philosophers and many cats. The wisdom of cats is infinitely superior.

HIPPOLYTE TAINE

Brainy basics

How smart are cats?

Cats are very hard to study scientifically. Not only do they tend to be less co-operative – which won't be news to a cat owner – they're also more prone to stress. Both factors combined make getting cats to engage with behavioural and cognitive experiments nigh on impossible. (Or perhaps they just choose to be above it all.) This means that there are still some areas of cats' brains that we know very little about.

A bundle of nerves

Cats have smaller brains compared to us and to dogs, but this isn't always an indicator of intelligence. They have more nerve cells in the visual areas of their brain than most mammals – this is part of the cerebral cortex, which is responsible for decision making, problem solving, planning, memory and language processing.

Add that fantastic memory – both long-term and short-term – and cats have quite a brain toolkit!

Super sleuth

Put your cat in an unfamiliar room and the first thing they'll do is investigate every nook and cranny – smelling, listening and taking everything in. This is thanks again to their well-developed cerebral cortex. By using their high-functioning brain to 'research' the room, they're gathering information and retaining it for future use; for example, if they're in danger they'll know where to run and hide. Curiosity doesn't kill your cat – it helps it to survive!

So why no service cats?

If cats are so clever, why don't we use them to sniff out contraband at airports or to help a blind person with their day-to-day life, like we do dogs? The short answer that cats don't like being enslaved! (Remember, you're not a cat owner – it's vice versa.) At times, they're impatient, intolerant, irritable – put simply, cats just aren't very social and would rather not help a human if it means moving. They're totally capable, just not willing! Which leads us on to...

Lack of empathy

Ever wondered what makes your cat so wonderfully self-centred? The answer is that the part of your cat's brain that manages feelings of empathy and social behaviour isn't as developed as it is in humans and dogs. This explains their intolerance of frustrating situations. It also casts a light on your cat's ultimate putdown... when it turns its back and walks away from you because they find you dreadfully boring. Cats are clever, but with a low social IQ!

PAWS FOR THOUGHT

Your cat's intellect is demonstrated by its ability to use information to solve problems. Scientists think their level of problem solving is roughly equivalent to that of a 2–3-year-old child.

What is intelligence?

It's very easy to say that someone is 'intelligent'; we normally mean that they're either very able academically or they just seem to 'get' everything. In reality, there's no single definition of what makes a person 'intelligent' and certainly not what makes them a 'genius' – and the same applies to cats. This is why we should never judge cats (or people for that matter) by what they can or can't do. So, what different types of intelligence do cats have?

Social cognition

Social cognition refers to the role that brain processes play in social interaction. How social is your cat? Do they want to interact with you? Cats are very independent, self-sufficient creatures so you might find

that your cat prefers time to itself – it doesn't make them socially backward, just, well... cat-like! To get an idea of your cat's level of sociability, consider whether they do the following:

- Greet you at the door when you come home.
- Come and sit next to or near you.
- Come when you call their name.
- Put themselves in a position where they know they'll be petted. (Just think of how they put themselves between you and your screen when your laptop is getting more attention than them!)

Training

Everyone thinks about training their dog, but very few think about training their cat to do anything beyond using the litter tray. Cats are often thought of as being untrainable, reinforced perhaps by the air of independence from us they like to maintain. However, it's possible to train a cat, but just like

dogs, some are more willing to be trained than others. Interestingly, when a cat is being trained, they seem to be motivated solely by treats – if, of course, they can be bothered. Unlike dogs, cats aren't interested in positive reinforcement through stroking and petting. Perhaps this shows how clever they are though – they know that there's more in it for them if treats are involved than a mere pat on the head!

Memory

From what we know – considering how hard it is to research cats! – cats have good memories. Their memory is believed to be around 200 times better than a dog's. A cat's short-term memory is approximately 16 hours. When it comes to long-term memory, their ability is much harder to determine. What we do know is that cats are very good at remembering people, particularly those they have a strong bond with or have been mistreated by in the past.

PAWS FOR THOUGHT

Cats understand physical causality. If there are several pieces of string, one with food attached to it, your cat will figure out which string they need to pull to get the food.

Object permanence

Object permanence is the ability to know that an object hasn't ceased to exist just because you can't see it. Surf the web and you'll find numerous videos of pets (mainly dogs of course) running around like fools trying to find their owners. For more on the importance of your cat's understanding of object permanence, see Now You See It... on page 78.

Quantity discrimination

Cats appear to have the ability to tell the difference between different quantities. (Just like when you're presented with a plate of cupcakes and you choose the biggest one with the most icing.) Research, although limited, suggests that cats can distinguish between quantities on a small scale. Not quite counting but useful nonetheless if your cat ever finds itself trapped in a fishmonger with a free choice!

These are just a few of the standard measures used with animals (and children) to see how their brains tick. By no means are they definitive and of course luck, randomness and how bored your cat is by you on that particular day should all be factored in.

Cats' brains: ten top facts

Cats are pretty incredible – and don't they like us to know it! Have you ever looked at your cat and wondered what they're thinking about behind that steely glare? They certainly don't give away as much as dogs do. Here are some fantastic facts to give you an insight into your cat's seemingly impenetrable mind.

1. A cat's brain takes up 0.9% of their total body mass. Compare that to humans (2%) and dogs (1.2%). Size really doesn't matter! Well, in comparison to other factors.

2. Cats learn through observation. As kittens they learn how to hunt, eat and groom themselves through watching their mothers. You'll find that they watch you in a similar way to pick up new skills. Cats weren't born knowing how to push open a door!

3. Your cat's brain has 91,000 gigabytes of data storage space and can process 6.1 trillion operations per second. That's faster than a typical 60GB iPad! Just don't ask us how anyone figured this out...

4. People and cats have identical sections in the brain that control emotion. Overall, a cat's brain is 90% similar to a human brain!

5. Female domestic cats tend to be right-pawed, while male cats use their left paw more frequently. And, yes, there has been a study done into this – with what objective we don't know!

6. Cats are VERY clever at getting what they want from us. A hungry cat will make an urgent cry or meowing sound in the 220–520 hertz range. As human babies usually cry between 300–600 hertz, humans find this very hard to ignore. Yes, your cat can manipulate the emotional response of your brain. Now who do you think is in control?

7. Research has found that cats can distinguish their own names and respond to them. So, yes, your cat is ignoring you on purpose.

8. Smell is important to young kittens, especially for finding their mother and her milk. They don't respond to auditory stimuli until 11–16 days old and visual stimuli until 16–21 days old.

9. As they get older, cats can develop Feline Cognitive Dysfunction Syndrome, which is very much like Alzheimer's disease in humans. It can lead to depression, confusion and anti-social behaviour.

10. Are cats really as independent as we think? A study in 2019 found that cats develop attachments much like humans and dogs do. They can become dependent on their humans and use them as a source of comfort.

Signs of super intelligence

So, you think your cat is a genius? We all like to think that our pets are superior to everyone else's. It's okay to be a proud parent! But you can be blinkered by love. Whilst some of the behaviour you see from your cat looks incredible, it could just be natural behaviour. What signs should you be looking out for to find out whether your cat really has got the cream when it comes to super intelligence?

Sign #1 – Great communication

Did you know that adult cats rarely meow to communicate with each other? Their vocalisations are entirely for the benefit of their subjects... sorry, we mean you, their owners. What's more, cats can change the sound of their meows in order to communicate different messages, for example: "I'm hungry", "Leave me alone, human" or "Please open this door before I scratch my way through it".

Cats can chatter, murmur, yowl and whisper to get what they want. If your cat uses its voice to communicate its different needs to you and you can clearly identify what they're trying to tell you, your cat is in the upper echelons of intelligence.

Sign #2 – Object permanence

This cognitive skill is mentioned time and time again as a sign of great intelligence in cats. It's so obvious to humans that an object that's been hidden hasn't simply disappeared that we take it for granted that our pets understand the same. Actually, it's not an easy concept for them. For more on object permanence and how to test your cat's understanding, see Now You See It... on page 78.

Sign #3 – Getting along with others

If your cat is able to get along well with humans and other animals, it's a good sign that they're of above average intelligence. It shows your cat's clever analytical mind at work – they've basically figured out that it's more likely to get them what they want. Well, you didn't think it was for your benefit, did you?

Sign #4 – Hunting prowess

A super clever cat is very skilled at catching things and breaking through all those years of domestication to show off their wild side! It doesn't matter whether they're catching the biggest frog in the garden (as a present for you, of course) or a feather on a stick, they're adept at hunting it down, there's a lot going on between those furry ears.

Your cat doesn't have to be good at ALL these things to be super intelligent. Like humans, every cat will have its strengths and its weaknesses. Those strengths might not even be listed above but that doesn't mean your cat is dumb. Just remember all those things they are good at, whether it be sensing when you're down and jumping onto your lap for cuddles, or their uncanny ability to hear from a distance of several miles as you approach their food caddy.

PAWS FOR THOUGHT

An interesting test is to watch a nature programme on TV with your cat. If they keep an intense eye on the 'prey', it's a good sign of intelligence.

Different breeds, different brains

It's common to think of different breeds of dog as having different levels of intelligence, but less so for cats. Perhaps it has something to do with them generally being so impenetrable! Like with dogs, the abilities of cats do vary according to their heritage. Rather than it being a case of 'stupid' or 'clever' breeds, it's far better to think of it as different breeds having different strengths – and weaknesses.

Top ten brainy breeds

1. **Siamese:** Incredibly inquisitive cats – a trait which often leads to them creating mischief! They respond to training better than most other breeds. Siamese cats crave attention so will readily let you know if they're unhappy or bored by caterwauling at you – certainly enough to motivate you to keep them entertained!

2. **Abyssinian:** Very confident cats that love interacting with their owners. They seem at their happiest when they are being mentally stimulated. Abyssinians have earned themselves the nickname 'Aby-grabbys' due to their tendency to try and take anything that's got your attention away from you so they can investigate it themselves.

3. **Bengal:** These cats love human interaction and communicating with their owners via their meows. They're also great explorers and enjoy jumping and climbing. Some owners claim that their cats have mastered the game of fetch. Bengal cats are brilliant with their paws and have a penchant for turning light switches on and off.

4. **Burmese:** Very sociable, enjoy chatting and love being at your side – this has led to them being described as 'dog-like' in their behaviour. Burmese cats are also good at living alongside dogs – another sign of intelligence. They can even learn to sit, roll over and fetch and love showing these tricks off. Attention-seekers? Oh yes.

5. **Cornish Rex:** Clever, inquisitive and love playing games (which they will demand you play at length). They're brilliant at finding things (so don't let them see you put things away), retrieving toys and playing fetch. They'll badger you incessantly for your attention.

6. **Savannah:** These cats are super, super active and quite 'wild' in comparison to other domestic cats. They need lots of play to keep them mentally stimulated – including going for a walk on a lead!

7. **Scottish Fold:** Easily bored, they adore playing whether it be with you (which they will demand you do at length) or solving puzzle toys. The more attention you give them, the more they thrive. They'll even sit and watch a movie with you, paying attention to what's going on on-screen.

8. **Japanese Bobtail:** These cats love playtime and solving puzzles and will talk to you with their chirrupy meows until the cows come home. They grow very fond of their owners and don't like being home alone for long. Luckily, bobtails travel well so you can just take them with you. A very adaptable cat, which gives a nod to their intelligence.

9. **Singapura:** Generally, very playful, outgoing and curious. They'll try to get involved in whatever you're doing, whether you like it or not. Singapura cats are also very physically active so you need to be prepared to exercise both their minds and their bodies if you want your furniture to remain intact!

10. **Turkish Van:** Despite being very clumsy, these cats love to jump and climb. They also have a fondness for water, which may manifest itself as an interest in your toilet bowl and your taps! Turkish Vans don't enjoy being picked up or cuddled but they do enjoy acrobatic games like catch and will therefore still demand your attention.

And the less clever breeds ...?

Lots of breeds make fantastic pets but aren't necessarily known for being the brightest bulb in the box. These include Birmans, Persians, Himalayans, exotic shorthairs and Ragdolls. However, some of these 'less smart' breeds are known for their docile, easy-going behaviour and affectionate nature. What's not to love about that even if it means your cat isn't a genius?

Cats are smarter than dogs. You can't get eight cats to pull a sled through snow.

JEFF VALDEZ

Cats can work out mathematically the exact place to sit that will cause most inconvenience.

PAM BROWN

Testing, testing

Spotting a clever kitten

It's hard to spot a clever kitten – in the first few weeks after they're born they're all wobbles and paws. And why worry about anything other their utter cuteness at this stage? Like human babies, your kitten is hardwired to learn so trying to figure out how smart they are is a moving target at this stage. However, you can look out for the signs of potential genius where a kitten is going above and beyond what's expected for their age.

Early days

If ever there's a time when kittens are at their bounciest and speediest, leaping, pouncing and stalking, it's now. Equally important to exploring their physical abilities, it's during the first seven weeks of their lives that kittens also learn about being social. They gradually discover their brothers and sisters, watching keenly what everyone else is doing in order to learn. Kittens also start to find out the difference between play biting and real biting and where to draw the line at inappropriate behaviour.

Is your kitten getting on well with its siblings? Is it learning from its mistakes? (i.e. Has it successfully figured out that the consequence of annoying its brother is a sharp paw swipe across the face?) If yes, it's a good sign that your kitten's brain is developing well.

Kittens shouldn't be separated from their mother and siblings at this stage. If they are, it can lead to poor learning skills, a lack of social skills and aggression.

Weeks 7–14

This is when your kitten's love of play really kicks off! (So pack away your valuables.) Anything they can chase or catch they will. If it moves, your kitten pounces. It's tremendous fun to watch them. This is an important stage in their learning where they really explore the world to find out what their brains and bodies can do. Start introducing lots of toys to stimulate their brains and you'll be laying solid foundations for the future. If your kitten is game for games, they're definitely climbing the cleverness rankings (as well as the curtains!).

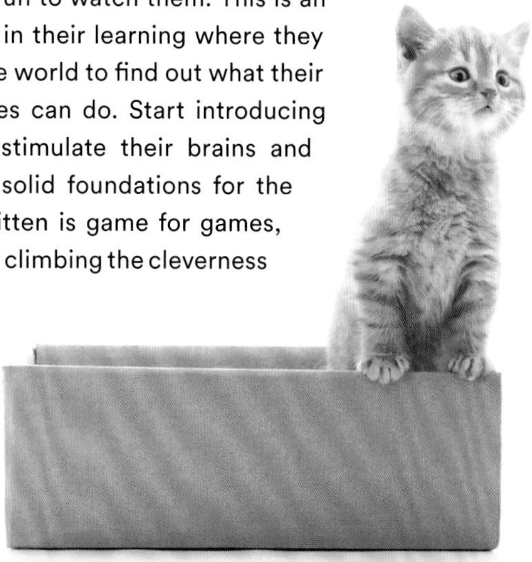

Months 3–18

As your kitten moves into adolescence, you'd be forgiven for thinking you've got a human teenager on your hands. Like teenagers, your kitten will start to push the boundaries as they discover what they can and can't get away with. They want to show you who's boss and will do their very best to challenge your authority – what do they say about how you never own a cat, but a cat owns you?

It's essential that you encourage your kitten to play in these early stages of their life. They are learning to 'be a cat'. Lots of stimulation will increase their physical co-ordination and social skills, but it will also boost their learning and brain power. You'll need to keep it up though – cats don't stop learning or being receptive to new experiences when they leave kittenhood. If your kitten doesn't seem to be as bright as its littermates, don't give up! You can teach an old cat new tricks.

PAWS FOR THOUGHT

Kittens that are handled for 15–40 minutes a day during their first seven weeks are more likely to develop larger brains and be better learners.

A cat can purr its way out of anything.

DONNA McCROHAN

Feline IQ tests

Tabitha likes kibble but not fish. She likes mutton but not lamb, and she likes Top Cat but not Garfield. Following the same rule, will she like scratches or tickles? First things first – close the tab on the Mensa website! You can't measure a cat's IQ like you would a human.

Why test your cat?

Cats are notoriously difficult to test, so why do we bother? There's nothing in it for your cat – they really couldn't care less and would be insulted that you'd even need to question their intellectual superiority. If you want to test your cat's IQ, you're most likely to be doing it because you already think they're a genius and want confirmation. There's no harm in trying to test your cat, but don't take it too seriously! A 'genius' in one area might not be a genius in another. It's all relative. IQ tests will measure certain areas of your cat's cognitive abilities, but they won't capture how brilliant your cat is at, for example, reading your emotions and knowing when to give you a cuddle.

Are IQ tests useful?

IQ tests only provide a narrow definition of intelligence. Human IQ tests focus on reading, writing, logic and analytical thinking – fantastic for assessing how someone might perform academically. But we all know extremely clever people who didn't do well at school or go to university and who have still been successful thanks to a skill or talent. IQ tests will measure certain areas of your cat's cognitive abilities, but they won't capture how brilliant your cat is at, for example, catching a feather on a stick or manipulating you into feeding them an hour early.

The standard tests

Go online or to your bookstore and you'll be spoilt for choice if you're looking for a cat IQ test. They're all fairly similar and assess the same standard areas: co-ordination, communication, social skills and reasoning. Here are some simple tests you can try with your cat, but do take them with a pinch of salt (your fickle cat will make it impossible to get accurate results) and remember that it's supposed to be fun!

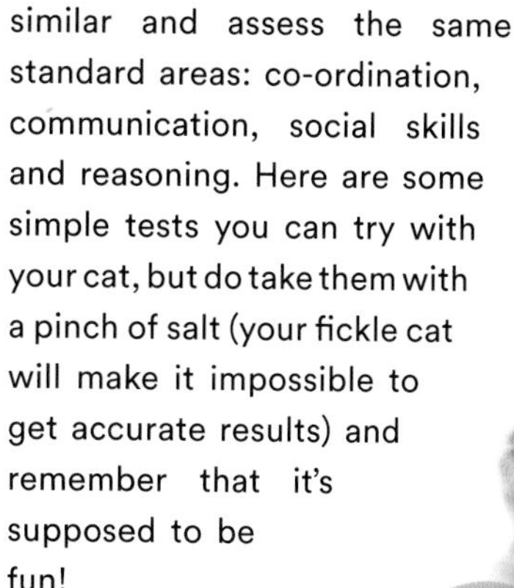

TEST 1 – PROBLEM SOLVING AND REASONING

If you have a clockwork toy for your cat – if you have, it's bound to be a mouse! – wind it up and set it going in full view of your cat. Orchestrate it so that the toy goes underneath a piece of furniture. What does your cat do? They'll most likely watch the toy's progress intently. But the test is when the toy disappears out of view, can your cat predict the position at which it will reappear? If they can, it's a very good indication of a high level of intelligence. They've used their observational skills to solve a problem – and if it was a real mouse sneaking out from underneath the sofa, it would be a goner!

TEST 2 – REASONING

An interesting mealtime test. Place an unopened packet or container of your cat's food near to their bowl. What does your cat do? If they look at the unopened food and then at you, and repeat that several times, you've got a very clever (and hungry) cat on your hands. They've used their reasoning to figure out that you're supposed to be serving them, hence THAT LOOK as they switch their gaze between you and the food. If your cat doesn't even bother to acknowledge the food, they're either not particularly smart or they've already eaten a huge meal!

TEST 3 – OBJECT PERMANENCE

Hide your cat's favourite toy behind something, for example a cushion or box, letting them see you hide it. Keep the area uncluttered so they can focus on that one toy. If your cat realises that the toy hasn't just vanished into thin air and tries to get to it, they are demonstrating how smart they are (equivalent to an 18-month-old child). If their interest is in no way piqued and their favourite toy is now essentially dead to them, your cat won't be taking up their place at university quite yet. (For more on object permanence see Now You See It... on page 78.)

TEST 4 – CAUSAL RELATIONSHIPS

Using a laser pointer, play with your cat for a few minutes. Then suddenly stop. If your cat looks at you or at your hand, then it's understood the basics of cause and effect. If your cat starts looking around for the red dot of the laser, it has failed to figure out that you're the source of the exciting dot of light.

TEST 5 – PROBLEM SOLVING

Gently place a towel or blanket over your cat, including their head. If they find their way out quickly, they're great problem solvers and haven't been completely flummoxed by what just happened to them. The longer it takes your cat to figure out that they can free themselves, the less you'd want find to yourself trapped anywhere with them. Regardless of how long it takes them to emerge from the blanket, be prepared for them to give you an almighty stare that conveys both hatred and how much of an idiot they think you are.

The challenges

Cats aren't like dogs. They're not so bothered about trying to please you or make you love them. Following commands and doing tricks bring dogs the attention and sense of belonging they crave. Cats are far more independent and wonder why they even need to bother showing you what they're capable of. "I'd love to perform a trick for you!" said no cat, ever.

Unfortunately, people therefore assume that cats are less intelligent that dogs. Humans tend to judge an animal's intelligence based on how much like a human it acts. Cats are uniquely cats, so seen through the lens of human expectations they're not always the sharpest crayons in the box.

Healthy cat, clever cat

A healthy body is key to a healthy mind whether you're a human or a cat. As your cat's servant – sorry, owner – it's up to you to make sure they get the right nourishment to boost their brain. You can't produce an Olympic athlete on burgers and fries; and you can't raise a feline Einstein on scraps from the trash.

Brain food for cats

Ideally, a good diet needs to start from kittenhood in order for your cat to develop a strong and healthy cognitive function. It can also reduce the risk and impact of degenerative brain diseases such as feline cognitive dysfunction syndrome (see page 112) as your cat grows older. But don't panic – it's never too late to start a healthy diet for your cat and the reap the benefits.

Getting your cat's diet right

A healthy cat needs to have a balanced diet that provides a variety of foods, including a range of proteins, fats, vitamins and minerals. When choosing your cat's food, choose food that's made with high quality ingredients, with as few artificial additives/ingredients as possible. Make sure too that the food is easily digestible. Despite their tendency for putting all sorts in their mouths whilst on the prowl outside, cats do have quite sensitive tummies.

Ditch the unhealthy, processed treats. You can swap in far healthier, nutrient-rich nibbles such as cooked sweet potatoes, pumpkin and carrots. (Holistic health practitioners also believe that vegetables provide a stabilising energy that focuses the mind.)

Fatty acids

Docosahexaenoic acid, or DHA, is a type of omega 3 fat proven to improve brain function and mental development (as well as being excellent for eyesight and joints). The brain is made up of mostly fat, so essential fatty acids like these are vital. DHA,

and the equally beneficial eicosapentaenoic acid (EPA), are commonly found in fish. Foods rich in DHA and EPA – like salmon and salmon oil – can improve learning abilities and short-term memory. Not all fish (for example farmed salmon) is of a high quality and good for cats; look out for high quality fish oils that contain wild-caught fish and seafood like herring, sardines, anchovies and mussels.

B vitamins

The role of B vitamins in improving cognitive processes is well-researched. Studies have found that cats getting a diet rich in nutrients, including B vitamins, are much brainier than those cats only fed the minimum levels.

Antioxidants

Antioxidants are important in the fight against free radicals, atoms that can harm the body's cells. Including antioxidants, such as Vitamins C and E, in your cat's diet helps protect against the free radicals that threaten brain function, particularly as your cat gets older.

Feline superfoods

Any supplementary foods should be fed to your cat in moderation – and start with small amounts just in case their tummy takes a turn! Here are five of the top superfoods to boost brainpower:

1. Broccoli – yes, broccoli! It's a hotbed of vitamins, minerals and antioxidants.
2. Chia seeds – a fantastic source of antioxidants and plant-based omega 3s.
3. Peas – vitamins B1, K and C, antioxidants.
4. Herring and sardines – omega 3 fatty acids, protein and Vitamin D.
5. Celery and carrots – contain luteolin, a compound found in fruit and veg that's been shown to reduce inflammation of the brain and restore memory function. (Cook until soft to avoid the risk of choking.)

PAWS FOR THOUGHT

Why not read to your cat whilst they're eating? Reading aloud to them can boost their brain power by activating neural pathways that keep the brain active and alive.

Brain games: counting for cats

Have you ever wondered if your cat can count? That would surely be a sign of genius! Research has found that cats do have an abstract idea of numbers up to 7. It's also thought that mother cats can detect when a kitten is missing from her litter (although it's hard to prove whether this is down to her ability to count or another sense, e.g. smell).

Whilst we don't know whether cats can count in the way we do, they do have a sense of quantity, i.e. they know the difference between 'bigger' and 'smaller'. This stems from their natural instinct – in the wild, they're more likely to try to catch the one big, fat, meaty pigeon than ten scrawny ones. Try this simple brain game with your cat and reach your own conclusions!

More or less?

Aim of the game: To find out whether your cat can tell the difference between a larger and a smaller quantity.

Step 1: Make sure your cat is hungry!

Step 2: Take three bowls and put a different quantity of food in each. Line them up.

Step 3: If your cat isn't already making a beeline for the food (which of course they will be!), call them and show them the cornucopia of food awaiting them.

Step 4: Observe to see which bowl of food your cat eats from. If they deliberate and settle on the bowl with the largest quantity of food, it's a good sign that they've got it going on up there. Not strictly counting but great mathematical estimation nonetheless!

If there is one spot of sun spilling on to the floor, a cat will find it and soak it up.

J. A .McINTOSH

Cats seem to go on the principle that it never does any harm to ask for what you want.

JOSEPH WOOD KRUTCH

The senses

Feline senses

If you rate your cat's intelligence based on their senses, it would far exceed the intelligence of us mere mortal humans. Like dogs, cats are blessed with extraordinary powers that, if you put them in capes, would make them superheroes. Knowing what your cat is capable of provides a good insight into what to expect of them and their remarkable brains.

Sight

- Cats' eyes let them down slightly in that they don't see in a great amount of detail. Objects further that 2–3 feet away will appear blurry.
- Cats have awesome vision in the dark and in near darkness. They need far less light to see than we do. And you know how your cat's eyes glow weirdly in the dark? That's

the special reflective layer at the back of the eyeball that draws more light in, allowing them to see in low-level light.

Hearing

- High frequency hearing. Cats can hear frequencies of up to 60kHz – compare that to humans (20kHz) and dogs (45kHz). Using their hearing alone they can accurately detect and locate their prey.

- Because of the sensitivity of their ears, cats respond much better to high-pitched sounds. So, whilst you might sound like an idiot talking to your cat in a squeaky voice, this is the most effective way to communicate with them.

- Swivelling ears. Cats can turn their ears independently through 180 degrees. They have a whopping 30 muscles for moving their ears.

Smell

- Your cat's most important sense. Why? See Taste below! If they can't smell it, they won't eat it.

- Because cats are born blind and deaf, their sense of smell ensures they survive as it leads them to their mother and her milk.

- Cats have 200 million – yes, TWO HUNDRED MILLION! – smell receptors. Us pathetic humans only have 5–6 million.

- Cats use their sense of smell to explore the world and to communicate with other cats and with us. Hence why they constantly rub their scent on you and the furniture.

Taste

- Cats were doing so well when senses were being dished out... and then they were only given 473 taste buds. Humans have 9,000!
- Thankfully, your cat's extraordinary sense of smell makes up for their lack of taste. It's the smell of food rather than the flavour that stimulates their appetite.
- Those taste buds detecting bitterness are your cat's most active. This helps protect them against consuming poisonous substances. If you've ever noticed a little black blob left after your cat has eaten a mouse, that's the mouse's gall bladder, which is filled with bitter bile – not to feline tastes! Yuck.

PAWS FOR THOUGHT:

Cats aren't very good at seeing colours in the way we do. They can tell the difference between greens and blue, but they have difficulty with red.

Sixth sense – fact or fiction?

Cats are renowned for their hint of other-worldliness and have been revered throughout history. Whether they're depicted on the back of a witch's broomstick or as black-furred crosser of paths, cats have that certain look in their eyes. Perhaps it's their mysterious 'sixth sense' that we find a little bit freaky. Are they geniuses and really do know more than we do or is it all just spooky coincidence?

Cats can detect human illness

FACT! Like dogs, cats seem to have an uncanny knack of spotting illness in humans. Illness has a distinctive smell (and taste) caused by chemical changes in the human body and this sparks the feline super senses. There are plenty of stories of cats all but donning a stethoscope; for example, the cat who massages its owner's head when they're getting the symptoms of a migraine, and the cat that climbed up into their owner's loft bed (a climb the cat had never made before) to wake them up before they slipped into a diabetic seizure. Cats have even been known to sense imminent death… so watch out when they start to pay you unusual attention!

Cats know when a storm is coming

FACT! Cats are indeed furry barometers but, again, there's no magic in it so don't expect them to tell you the winning lottery numbers. Cats can smell the increase in ozone in the air that precedes a storm – even humans are capable of this but not to the same level as the uber sensitive noses of cats. Their whiskers and fur also pick up the increase in electricity in the air so watch out for their fur standing slightly on end. Your cat may also rub their ears as the change in air pressure affects their inner ear. Time to dig out your umbrella.

Cats can predict earthquakes and eruptions

FACT! But sorry, it's not some oracle-like sight that they have. With their vibration-detecting whiskers and sensitive paws, cats can pick up the very early signs of an earthquake or volcanic eruption through the very subtle foreshocks. As the vibrations get stronger, cats become increasingly agitated, which is the point at which we start to notice a change in their behaviour. In the case of volcanic eruptions, cats' incredibly sensitive noses can also detect the release of chemicals into the air that precede the eruption. Clever!

Cats can see ghosts

HMMMM. Does your cat startle for no reason? Do they stare at 'empty' spaces for a long period of time? They may have seen a ghost, but it's more likely that their sensitive super senses are simply picking up things in the natural world that our dull senses don't. So, fact or fiction? This is entirely down to whether or not you believe in the supernatural.

I had been told that the training procedure with cats was difficult. It's not. Mine had me trained in two days.

BILL DANA

Working together

Can you create a genius?

We've all read about parents who hothouse their kids to get them to the top of the class. And it's guaranteed that you know someone who's a 'tiger mom', pushing their child to be the very best at EVERYTHING. Can you (and should you) do the same with your cat? With a nudge in the right direction, is your cat a genius just waiting to happen?

How cats learn

If you want to encourage your cat to be as clever as possible, you need to understand how they learn. Armed with this information you can maximise their brain power. Cats are very fast learners (when they can be bothered!) and, like children, learn constantly even when you think they're not looking or listening. Oh, if cats could talk...

Natural instinct still plays a huge part in the behaviour of domestic cats. With their finely tuned ears and noses, cats are also adept at understanding the world through their senses, collecting experiences and adding them to their brain bank.

Association

One of the ways that cats learn is through association, which basically means they're very good at putting two and two together. Learning through association is akin to habit – it happens through repetition and positive reinforcement. For example, if every time your cat climbs onto your lap you lavish it with attention, they'll soon learn to expect this (if they like cuddles of course – if they don't, they'll learn to avoid you equally quickly!). What this also means is that you need to be careful not to inadvertently teach your cat bad behaviour.

The most common association you'll notice them make is of course related to food. You can gently shake your cat's food container at a distance of 5km and they'll be at your feet in an instant, knowing that their dinner is on the way.

Making the most of positive associations is a great way to help your cat learn. For example, if your cat is unnerved by small children (who isn't?!), give them (the cat, not the child) lots of attention and a few treats and they'll start to associate children with good times and their anxiety will reduce.

Observation

Cats love to stare. Sometimes in quite an unsettling way. They are taking in an awful lot of information about the world around them. One of the things they pick up is cause and effect; for example, if your cat watches you open a door over and over, they'll figure out exactly what a door handle does and give it a go themselves. If you think your cat is a genius because they can open a door, they've learnt everything they know from you!

Brain training

Brain training is a way of exercising the mind and improving cognitive skills. Whole books have been written about brain training cats and it's a trend with humans too – just think how sudokus and crosswords are recommended for staving off brain decline. We've not got a cat-friendly sudoku for you, but you'll find a selection of brilliant brain games dotted throughout this book.

Top tips

If you want to get the best out of your cat's amazing brain, these are the things to remember:

- Reward, reward, reward: Cats are out for themselves. If they can reap a reward from doing something they will. If they can be bothered.
- Repetition: Cement associations in your cat's brain and they'll pick up good (and bad) habits in a flash. Be consistent – they need to know what to expect and won't relish surprises. If they usually get a treat for a trick, they won't be impressed by an ear rub instead.
- Most of all: be kind, be loving and be patient!

PAWS FOR THOUGHT

Cats are solitary territorial creatures, so they won't see you as part of the 'pack' in the way dogs do. Whatever they learn is very much for their own benefit, not to please you!

Communication skills

Being good at communicating their needs to you is a very good sign of your cat's intelligence. But it's a two-way street. You need to be good at understanding what they're trying to say! That's how you'll get the best out of their finely honed feline brain and encourage them to learn more and learn faster. How can you tune in to your cat's wavelength?

It's all in the eyes

You already know how powerful your cat's stare is. One laser beam glare and you're crying for mercy. It's what cats are good at! However, there's much more subtlety involved than you think. Cats use eye contact very differently to humans and their eyes are constantly working to monitor their environment so that they're ready for anything.

Building a bond of trust with your cat is essential if you want to work together to engage their brain. If your cat gives you slow, languid blinks (otherwise known as 'cat kisses'), they are showing you their trust and affection. You can blink back at them to return the sentiment but don't be surprised if they react with indifference or fear – that's cats: never beholden to you and with moods that change like the wind!

Ready to learn and play

If you want to stimulate your cat's brain through play or to teach them a trick, use their body language to judge whether they're in the mood. Look out for these signs that your cat is feeling focused:

- Wide eyes and narrow pupils.
- Tail up – an invitation to play.
- Ears and whiskers pricked and facing forward.
- Lots of scent rubbing – particularly around your legs if you're the object of focus.
- Body and tail low to the ground – this stalking posture signifies play-hunting mode.

Spot these signs and it's a good time to start interacting with your cat. If you don't, you'll find your cat knocking your glasses off or sitting on your keyboard – the negative attention you'll give them is, in a cat's mind, better than no attention at all!

When not to engage

Do you learn well and perform at your best when you're angry, scared, frustrated or anxious? No. The same applies to cats. Interacting with your cat to engage their brain will be completely useless if they're not in the mood. Here's what to look out for... and then keep away until your cat is ready:

- Tail flicking from side to side: feeling VERY irritated.
- Tail arched: feeling aggressive.
- Standing tall, rigid, puffing up fur and generally trying to look bigger: feeling angry and defensive.
- Ears moving around rapidly, whiskers drawn back, tail low to ground, dilated pupils: feeling anxious.

PAWS FOR THOUGHT

After decades of study, scientists have concluded that cats have facial expressions. However, cats have learnt that us humans respond better to meows than the subtle positioning of whiskers!

Cat talk

The more your cat talks to you, the more you'll tune into the subtle (and not so subtle) differences between the sounds they make. There could be one meow for "Hello", one for "Let me out" and another for "Quit chasing me with that feather". Your cat is driven by need – mainly food – but that doesn't mean that every noise they make is a demand to be fed (although of course they won't say "No" if you do feed them).

If your cat is clever, they'll learn how to get exactly what they want from you. For example, does your cat meow at you whilst you're reading a book? With a meow that's incessant and gets increasingly loud? Do you pick them up and cuddle them and the meowing stops? Do you do that every time they give you that same meow? Ah ha. And there you have it. You're putty in your cat's paws!

Last but not least: you...

Your cat will pick up on your body language very easily, especially if you're feeling angry or frustrated. If you want to nurture their intelligence and encourage them to play, you need to keep calm and cool. Losing your temper because they won't do a trick is not only cruel, it'll ruin your relationship with your cat. Be patient and remember that 99 times out of 100, your cat will do what they want to do, not what you want them to!

Brain games: target training

Target training – basically, teaching your cat to touch an object – forms the basis of lots of tricks. It's a simple but impressive way to get your cat's brain working and their IQ growing.

Nose nudge

Aim of the game: As the title of the brain game says, teach your cat to nudge an object with its nose.

Step 1: Choose your object. It could be your hand, a stick or a toy – whatever you like. Show it to your cat. (Don't expect them to look too interested at this stage but you could provide a bit of a bribe/incentive by rubbing one of their favourite treats on it.)

Step 2: Hold the object about half an inch from your cat's

nose. If they pay it some attention, reward them with a treat and a tickle in their favourite spot.

Step 3: Repeat Step 2 until you think your cat understands what's expected of them. If the aim of the game has clicked, they'll know to nudge the object as soon as it's placed near their nose.

Next steps: You can try gradually moving the object further away to stretch your cat's abilities. It's also wise to phase out the treats as a reward or you'll end up with a clever but chubby kitty.

Use your imagination to think of ways to make the most of target training and your cat's cleverness. Could you teach them to ring a bell with their nose when they want to be let out? Or perhaps to gently nudge you awake in the morning with their nose rather than swiping you around the face with their claws?! Perhaps a step too far...

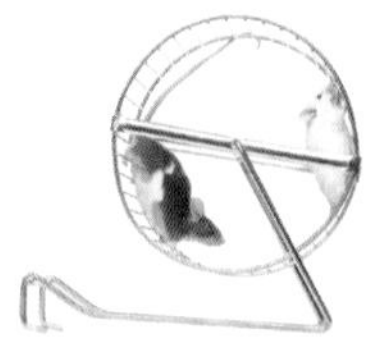

Social skills

Cats aren't social beasts and prefer the solitary life. Humans, on the other hand, are very social in comparison – annoyingly so if you're a cat. It's a wonder that cats and humans manage to live in the same space. It's like being the office introvert and finding that you're sharing a room with Mouthy Martin from Marketing at the annual company conference. If your cat appears to have ANY social skills, they're cleverer than the average moggy.

No, no, no…

Does your cat understand the word "No"? Do you tell them "No" until you're blue in the face, but it doesn't stop them doing anything or deter them from repeating bad behaviour? Don't be too hard on them as there is a reason for this. Unlike dogs, cats struggle to process social feedback. They can't connect your reaction with their action – all they see is you trying to randomly scare them. So, if you genuinely think your cat understands the word "No", they're displaying intelligence unlike most cats – they're a genius!

Bonding with your cat

Even if it sometimes feels like it's all take and no give, it's possible to build a strong bond of love and trust with your cat. Bonds are two-way and your cat will begrudgingly permit that if there's also something in it for them!

- Make time to groom your cat. Through trial and error, you'll soon learn where your cat does and doesn't like being touched. They usually respond well to rhythmical brushing – knowing what to expect means there are no surprises and your cat can relax into it.
- Your cat needs to associate you with the good things in life! They need to know that you can provide affection, security and, of course, food. We know that mistreatment sticks firmly in a cat's memory so always be kind and patient and they'll trust you to the end of the world.

- Never chase your cat around, no matter how desperate you are for a cuddle. Let them come to you. It might feel like an eternity with some cats, but they'll eventually relent.
- Learn the signs that your cat is telling you to back off... and listen! Flattened ears, twitching tail, dilated pupils – respect them and they'll respect you.

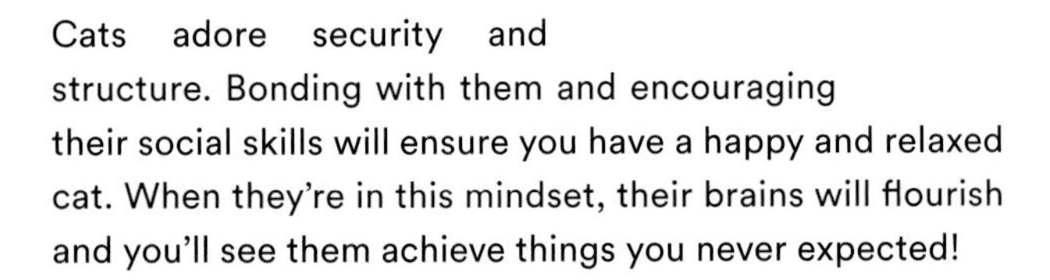

Cats adore security and structure. Bonding with them and encouraging their social skills will ensure you have a happy and relaxed cat. When they're in this mindset, their brains will flourish and you'll see them achieve things you never expected!

PAWS FOR THOUGHT

Despite having limited social skills of their own, cats can help children with autism improve their social skills. Having responsibility for a cat lets children learn strong interpersonal skills such as sharing and empathy.

Famous geniuses and their cats

Cats can be supremely clever and majestic, but what of their owners? What have feline muses brought to the lives of our famous artists, scientists and writers? We like to think that every ground-breaking discovery or work of art is all down to cats...

Nikola Tesla

Story has is that Telsa was inspired to investigate electricity after noticing sparks whilst stroking his pet cat, Macak. You have to wonder quite how static that poor cat's fur was!

Salvador Dali

Spanish surrealist painter Dali owned a cat that was just as exotic as its owner. No ordinary cat, Dali's feline companion, Babou, was an ocelot. Ocelots are a dwarf leopard breed native to Central and South America. Dali and Babou even went out to parties together!

Ernest Hemingway

Writer Hemingway absolutely adored cats, at one point owning up to 23. His love of cats was sparked when he was given a 6-toed cat by a ship's captain. The cat was named Snowball and Hemingway's house (now a museum) is home to over 40 of Snowball's descendants!

Samuel Johnson

Samuel Johnson compiled the first English language dictionary in 1755. His beloved cat, Hodge, is immortalised in a statue outside the author's home in London. The statue also features Hodges' favourite food – oysters. Johnson would go out and buy them specially for him.

Edwin Hubble

Hubble was an American astronomer whose work papers were often sprawled over by his part-Persian cat, Nicolas. Such was Nicolas' dominance, Hubble referred to his home as 'Nicolas' Estate'. The house was full of pipe cleaners as they were Nicolas' favourite toy.

Florence Nightingale

Nightingale, the pioneer of modern nursing, far preferred her work and her cats over friends. She is said to have owned around 60 cats over the course of her lifetime. Evidence of their presence can be found on her writing where they left inky little paw prints!

Edgar Allan Poe

Poe was a writer best known for his short stories and poetry, which were often dark and macabre. He claimed that his beloved cat Catterina played a big part in the creative process and he called her his 'literary guardian'. If you read Poe's short story The Black Cat, you'd be forgiven for thinking that he hated cats!

Freddie Mercury

Freddie Mercury adored his cats. When away on tour he would regularly phone home to talk to them. Cats can't hold phones so luckily Mercury's long-time friend Mary Austin would hold the cats up to the receiver. Aww!

In ancient times cats were worshipped as gods; they have not forgotten this.

TERRY PRATCHETT

Memory

Marvellous memory

Think 'memory' and 'cats' and you probably think of Grizabella belting a tune out on a Broadway stage. But back in the real world, your cat's memory skills are a good indication of how clever they are. It's not an easy thing to study, but researchers have concluded that cats have good memories – 200 times better than dogs! The question is, does your cat have a memory great enough to make it a genius?

Short-term memory

A cat's short-term memory is approximately 16 hours. Short-term memory is what allows us to store information for a short time and use it. In humans, a good short-term memory can make you better at maths, reading, language and learning generally. It's even been argued that short-term memory is more important than IQ when it comes to academic success. Yet another reason not to bother giving your cat an IQ test to find out if they're a genius!

Long-term memory

Long-term memories are those memories that are stored for a long time and can still be accessed by your cat – particularly those created by events in a cat's younger days. For example, if a cat is mistreated, that memory gets firmly embedded and can resurface years later. If your cat is scared of people wearing glasses or of loud noises it could be related to something traumatic that has happened in the past.

Cats have very good long-term memory skills when it comes to remembering people. They are good at recognising and differentiating between faces – and probably have a good recollection of smells too. There are plenty of heart-warming stories about cats that get separated from their owners only to remember them when they're reunited years later. Search on the internet and prepare to have your heart melted...

Episodic memory

You'll have noticed (how could you fail to?) that your cat pesters you for food at the exact same time each day. They are very sensitive to routine and will remember what's supposed to be happening at a particular time based on their experience (and they won't let you forget it) – this is called 'episodic' memory. Sometimes this may also be their ability to learn through association: as soon as they see you walk even remotely in the direction of their food source or slightly rustle a bag, they're on it. But episodic memory is different as it doesn't rely on sensory stimuli – it's purely your cat recalling where, when and what.

Does my cat have a super memory?

Your cat may demonstrate the basics above, but can they stretch their powers of recall into the realm of genius? Try these easy tests to find out.

Test 1: Short-term memory

The best tests for pets always seem to involve food! Find four small containers under which you can hide a treat. Let your cat watch you hide the treat under one of the containers. Pick them up and give them a cuddle for a few seconds so that they don't immediately go for the treat. Put them back down again and see if they can remember which container the prize is hidden under. If they go straight for it, your cat has an excellent short-term memory. You can extend the time you keep them from beginning their search to challenge them further.

When this test was conducted by researchers, they found that most cats in the experiment had difficulty finding the treat after 30 seconds. If your cat does better than this, watch out, you may have a genius on your hands! Who knows what they're plotting...

Test 2: Long-term memory

This test is the same as the above but even more challenging. Follow the same process, but this time remove your cat from the room for 5 minutes. What do they do when they're back in the room? Again, the quicker they find the treat, the better their long-term memory. You can try extending the time they're out of the room to find their limits. Try not to put the treat in the same place each time or they'll very cleverly catch on!

PAWS FOR THOUGHT

Kittens are at their most impressionable aged 2–7 weeks old. If a kitten has no interaction with humans during this time, it's unlikely that they'll ever trust them.

Now you see it...

Your partner has put a shopping bag in the trash. Does that mean the ridiculously expensive item of clothing they've just purchased doesn't exist? No. You're clever because you know that because something has vanished, it doesn't mean it doesn't exist. You understand object permanence. It's a concept that can also be used to measure your cat's intelligence.

Object permanence

Object permanence is the ability to recognise that an object doesn't simply vanish or stop existing if you can't see it. It's not an ability that every species is automatically born with. In humans, babies develop an understanding of object permanence by around 9 months of age, if not earlier. It's considered a vital and healthy sign of cognitive development.

Cats appear to have a good understanding of the concept – not surprising as once through kittenhood they develop the cognitive abilities of a human toddler. For cats, it's a vital part of being a hunter. If they gave up on a chase every time their prey disappeared behind something, they'd be one very frustrated and hungry kitty.

Take the test

It's very easy to test your cat's prowess in object permanence. And it's a good fun way to watch your cat's brain ticking!

Start by choosing an object that you know your cat is interested in. It could be a treat (winner!) or one of their favourite toys. Let your cat see the object then hide it behind something, for example a cushion or box. What does your cat do? If they immediately try to remove or navigate the obstruction to get to the object, their understanding of object permanence is top notch. If they sit waiting for it to reappear in the place they last saw it, that's equally clever as it shows they know it hasn't permanently stopped existing.

But what if your cat simply walks away and doesn't try to find the object? It could be that they're simply not in the mood to play – it's always a good idea to check they are before you embark on anything like this. On the other hand, their disinterest could mean than they've not grasped object permanence and they may be a little... ahem... 'slower' than the average moggy. But never fear: object permanence is just one measure of your cat's intelligence – they could be an exceptional genius in a different area.

The smart cat doesn't let on that he is.

H.G. FROMMER

Brain games: classic tricks

Don't let anyone tell you that your cat can't be trained in the same way a dog can. Okay, so it can be a little harder – they don't like being told what to do and they control how they spend their time, not you. But it can be done. So teach your cat to sit, stay and roll over better than any measly mutt. And, of course, they'll do it with more grace and infinitely more finesse!

Sit!

Aim of the game: Just like it says on the tin, teach your cat to sit on command. As with most brain games that involve a treat-shaped reward, best done when your puss has a rumbling tummy.

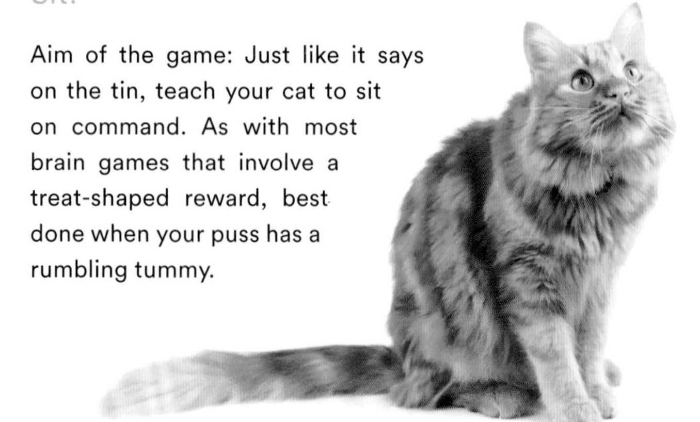

Step 1: Trouble your cat for their precious attention and tell them to "Sit" using an encouraging tone of voice. As you say "Sit", hold a treat above their eye level and above head height.

Step 2: Here comes the clever bit... Your cat will (well, should) tip their head back to follow the treat and thereby need to sit down to keep their balance. Immediately as their butt moves towards the floor, repeat the word "Sit" and reward with them with a well-earned treat. It's all about making that association between the command, the action and the reward.

Step 3: Repeat and repeat, at least until your cat gets bored with playing ball. The association will gradually be established in their brain. All being well, your cat will eventually learn to sit when you give the command and raise your hand, even when there's no treat in sight.

Fetch!

Aim of the game: Another classic dog game that your cat is perfectly capable of mastering. Cats are skilled retrievers – just think of all those lovely half-dead gifts they bring you from the garden. But don't use a

poor mouse for this game – a favourite toy that's easy for your cat to carry will do.

Step 1: Holding a treat, call your cat, throw the toy and say "Fetch". As long as they're in a playful mood, your cat should go for the toy. When they let you take the toy from them, it's time to reward them with a treat. Like with "Sit", you're teaching them to associate an action with a reward.

Step 2: This bit may take some time so be patient. Providing you practice and repeat the game, your cat should gradually start to bring the toy back to you leaving you to put your feet up!

Shake!

Aim of the game: Teach your cat to shake paws with you. Simple but heart melting – and it looks impressive too.

Step 1: Get your cat's attention by showing them you've got a tasty treat in your hand. It's when you close your

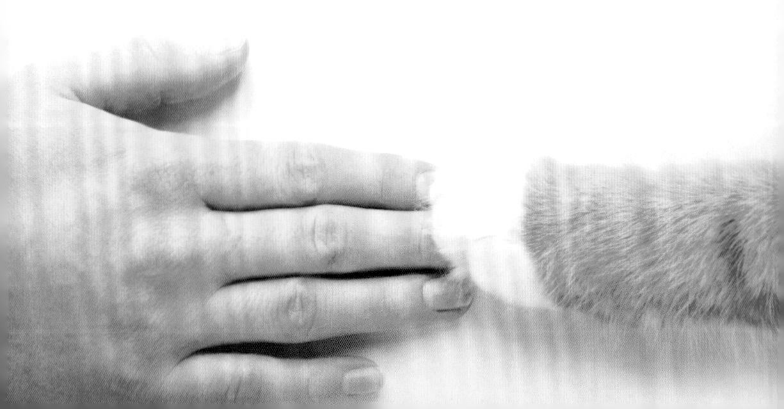

hand that the magic (hopefully!) happens. To try and get to the hidden treat, your cat should lift their paw up to your hand, giving the semblance of a handshake. As they do, say the verbal cue "Shake".

Step 2: Practice and practice until your cat associates the word 'shake' and you holding your hand out with the action of raising their paw. Once they are consistently 'greeting' you, you can phase out the treats. Job done!

Remember that cats aren't all that keen on having their paws touched so be patient and let them explore their comfort zone. There's no rush – brain games are great for stimulating your cat's brain but shouldn't be stressful.

PAWS FOR THOUGHT

Cat paw pads contain large concentrations of nerve receptors. Cats feel texture, pressure and vibrations through their pads, which helps them judge how active and close their prey is. However, their pads are also very sensitive to temperature, pressure and pain.

Cats rule the world.

JIM DAVIS

Unlock your cat’s potential

Keeping your cat stimulated

Keeping your cat's brain active is an ongoing job, especially if you think you've got a bright puss. Don't assume they can simply make their own entertainment when they're outdoors; whilst their natural behaviours do kick in, even those will be dulled if your cat's brain is generally under stimulated. There's plenty you can do to keep your cat's intellect active and boost their brain power – it's not complicated but you do have to put the time and effort in.

My cat is fine!

Then you're already doing a great job! But are you sure you're doing enough? Could you do more? Don't risk not nurturing their genius. Watch out for these signs that your cat is bored:

- Obsessive grooming and shedding lots of fur.
- Scratching (or destroying!) furniture.
- Aggression.

- Changes in their sleeping patterns – particularly excessive sleeping.
- Changes in toilet habits, for example going outside of their normal place/litter tray.
- Overeating or undereating.

It's always worth checking with your vet that there are no medical reasons for the above behaviour. If your cat gets the all-clear, it's time to think about what you can do to keep them more mentally active.

How to challenge your cat's brain

Don't panic and over complicate matters! There's no need to hire a tutor. Keep it simple, manageable and fun and both you and your cat will reap the rewards.

- Interactive games. Pet stores are full of games and puzzles to keep your cat's brain ticking. Start out with cheap and easy – it's tempting to overspend and then be disappointed when your cat shows no interest. You could even steal the simplest ideas and recreate them at home using household items or trusty cardboard toilet rolls.

- A breath of fresh air. Providing your cat isn't a house cat, make sure they get plenty of opportunity to go outside, stretch their legs and explore. The great outdoors will stimulate all their senses and encourage them to express their natural instinct to stalk and hunt.

- Rotate their toys. If your cat enjoys playing with toys, try swapping the toys around so they don't get bored with the same ones. And it saves you money too – old toys miraculously transform into new toys every couple of weeks!

- Brain games and tricks. We've done the hard work for you! Throughout this book you'll find brain games and tricks to try out with your cat. Even if they don't master them, you'll still be stimulating their brain in the process.

The benefits: your cat

Keeping your cat's brain stimulated has mental and physical benefits:

- Banishes boredom. In many pets, boredom leads to undesirable and destructive behaviour. As much as your cat loves lying around just sleeping and chilling, if they get bored, they'll get stressed. For a bright and playful cat, that's like shutting Einstein in a room without a pen and paper!

- Encourages natural behaviours. Give a cat the choice between chasing a bird and sitting on top of a radiator, they'll probably choose the latter. The more you can encourage play, the more their natural skills and inquisitiveness will emerge.
- Boosts their ability to learn, potentially unlocking that hidden streak of genius!
- Mental stimulation (and the accompanying boost to physical exercise) results in a far happier, more engaged existence for your cat. (And we can learn from that too!)

The benefits: you

Let's face it, cats are selfish so don't feel bad if you want to get something out of this too. How can a quick-witted, brainy cat benefit you?

- The more you interact and play with your cat, the better you'll get at reading their behaviour and understanding their body language. This means better, more effective communication between the two of you.
- Spending time with your cat and being able to read their needs will strengthen your bond. You'll feel more loved (albeit briefly, i.e. when your cat feels like endowing you with that feeling). Your cat will feel more safe and secure and this is needed for their faculties to flourish.

- The better you work together, the more likely it is that your cat will respond to the rules and boundaries you set. Perhaps keeping them off the kitchen counter so they don't dribble on your dinner isn't a pipe dream after all.
- A happy, stress-free cat means a happy, stress-free owner! And vice versa of course.

Cats and depression

Sadly, cats can experience depression. They don't experience it in the same way as humans do, but it does have an equally detrimental effect on their wellbeing. According to experts, pain and physical illnesses can cause symptoms like depression so it's always worth getting your cat checked out by a vet. The signs of depression to look out for mirror those listed above in relation to boredom.

Cats can become depressed because they are stressed. Often, it's quite simple to eliminate whatever factor is making them stressed. Perhaps they just don't have anywhere to hide from noisy human housemates. It could be that something in your daily routine has changed and that's unsettling them (cats are sticklers for structure). Another major factor is a lack of mental and physical stimulation. If you do notice warning signs, have a think about what more you could be doing with your cat to keep those wonderful cogs in their brain well-oiled. Small changes make all the difference and can reap big rewards.

Words and whiskers

It won't surprise you that cats know far more than we think they do. This includes vocabulary. They learn through association and observation so it's inevitable that your cat will come to understand what particular words mean – especially if it means a reward for them! It might not take a particularly clever cat to learn a few words, but how far above and beyond does your cat need to go to be called a genius?

The benchmarks

The jury is out on how many words a cat can learn. Some experts think it's as many as 50, whilst others estimate a more conservative 15–25. What we do know is that – in true keeping with typical cat behaviour – they're very good at learning words that are beneficial to them. They'll pick up useful words like 'dinner', 'garden' and 'food' very easily, but will turn their back on you if you ask them where the TV remote is.

Why teach vocabulary to your cat?

Many of the words cats learn are simply picked up through the course of everyday life with you. However, it can be useful to teach them specific words so that you can communicate effectively with each other, whether that be to enforce rules and boundaries ("Down!") or to keep them safe ("Stay!"). But don't expect them to behave like a dog. A dog can learn over 150 words and will do that to please you – a cat's motivation is very different, they only want to please themselves.

We may never really know how extensive a cat's vocabulary is and they would probably like to keep it that way. That said, if you do find your cat obeying commands like a dog (without showing you their butt in disdain), you can be confident your cat is a genius.

Getting started

As tempting as it may be to discuss quantum physics with your cat, they're most likely to remember concrete

words they can associate with an object, rather than an abstract concept. They'll get 'bowl' but 'high energy particles smasher' will be met with a nonchalant yawn. If you're teaching your cat new words (or indeed anything), they're most likely to listen and respond to a soft, calm, higher pitched voice. In fact, they're more receptive to the tone you use than the content. Even though it might sometimes appear like they're not listening, studies have confirmed that cats do pay attention to us!

Teach a phrase

Purposefully teaching your cat a phrase is a great way of getting their brain working – and of discovering whether your cat has genius potential. Don't expect miracles and, as always, patience and time are your friends!

Step 1: Decide what phrase you want to teach your cat. What might be useful? Don't aim for a full sentence or you're doomed to fail. Try something like 'chair' or 'time for dinner'.

Step 2: Every time you say your chosen phrase, produce a favourite treat. If you're teaching your cat to sit on a particular chair, let them have the treat when they jump onto the chair. (Remember that your cat needs to feel it's getting something out of this circus!) What you're doing is creating the association in your cat's brain: words + action = treats.

Step 3: ... is of course PRACTICE, PRACTICE, PRACTICE! And make sure you're consistent.

Step 4: If you've decided to teach your cat 'time for dinner', you may even find they start talking to you. Really. Bear with us here... If you delay dinner time by an hour, your cat will become impatient. Listen carefully to their meows and pay attention to the tone and the rhythm of the syllables. You might find that they're mimicking you saying "Time for dinner"!

Step 5: If Step 4 has been a success, this next step is for the genius cats who have nailed it. Next time your cat wants to sit on the chair or have their dinner, they'll ask you. Yes, they'll speak to you!

PAWS FOR THOUGHT

It's thought that cats recognise the pattern of a word rather than a unique word. Try calling them using a word that sounds like their name (e.g. "Dirty" rather than "Bertie") and you'll find they respond in the same way as if you'd called their actual name.

Dogs are high on life.
Cats need Catnip.

MISSY DIZICK & MARY BLY

I love both the way a dog looks up to me and a cat condescends to me.

GLADYS TABER

Every cat is unique

Clever cats: the downsides

Whether you think your cat is a genius or not doesn't determine the fun and love you'll share with them. As a cat owner, you know that all cats are wonderful! However, if your cat is super bright it can be hard work at times. You need to keep them on their toes – and they'll certainly be keeping you on yours. It's important to be aware of the potential problems and challenges if you want to ensure your cat stays healthy and happy.

Did you know?

- Clever cats often have lots of energy. As well as extra mental stimulation, they'll also need lots of additional physical activity. Bear this is mind if they're stuck indoors all day whilst you're at work. They'll need some way of stretching their muscles, for example a cat tree.

- A clever cat will have mastered the art of hunting prey. Be prepared for death and destruction in the backyard and plenty of half dead 'gifts' arriving in your home.

- If your cat thrives on play, contact and mental stimulation, the impact of not getting those needs met will hit them hard. You need to keep the momentum going, which can be tiring. See Keeping Your Cat Stimulated (page 88).

- Clever cats will easily get bored with your attempts to play. Mix up the games and toys so that you're not endlessly doing the same thing with your cat. Variety is the catnip of life!

What your clever cat needs from you

All cats need lots of your love and attention. Whether they give you any affection in return is totally up to them! Think of your feline genius as like having a precocious child; they need to be constantly stimulated but rely on you to put in all the hard work to make it happen. To keep up with your cat, you need to tick these boxes:

- A whole lot of energy. You need to keep up with your cat's demands. You'll start to wonder who the owner is and who's the pet.
- Imagination. A clever cat will bore easily so keep things interesting. As much as cats love familiarity and routine, keep things spiced up and fresh, especially when it comes to toys. You may even find you become an absolute whizz at knocking up creations made solely of empty yoghurt pots.

- An ability to read your cat's body language. A clever cat knows how to communicate with you, but you need to know what to look out for. Not only will this build a strong bond of trust, you'll also be able to spot when your cat is getting bored and you need to up your entertainment game.

- Patience. Giving your cat a lot of your time can be frustrating when they aren't reciprocating your enthusiasm. Bear in mind that your cat is a cat and their social skills are pretty terrible.

PAWS FOR THOUGHT

A bright cat can be a little bit naughty at times. Never punish unwanted behaviour – it won't prevent it – all it does is increase your cat's stress levels and teaches them that you're threatening. Instead, focus on rewarding positive behaviour.

Brain games: beat loneliness

Not all brain games require you to get involved on your hands and knees. You can nurture your cat's streak of genius with more standoffish, but equally effective, games. The games below are particularly good to use if you're out of the house during the day. Whilst cats pride themselves on their independence, they still get bored and lonely in those few minutes they're not asleep.

Treasure hunt

- Aim of the game: Keep your cat physically and mentally active with a scavenger hunt around the house. It's great to keep them busy when they're home alone.

Step 1: Split your cat's normal bowl of food up into small portions and hide it around the house. Tempting as it is,

don't be too clever or ambitious with your hiding places – you want your cat to find the food or you'll be discovering it yourself months later.

Step 2: Put some of the food in more obvious places so that your cat gets the idea that it's game on. Once they've cottoned on, their amazing nose will get to work and they'll be off.

Step 3: Too easy for your cat? Use your judgement. If you think they can cope with more difficult hiding places, give it a try. Their noses will locate the food, but the next level means putting their problem-solving skills into action. If your cat is a genius, this shouldn't pose a problem.

Create a cat-tastic home

Creating a playful environment for your kitty will not only keep their brain and body active whilst you're out, it will also save your furniture from any boredom scratching. DIY is just as good as shop bought so there's no need to spend a fortune. Your cat will find these simple ideas irresistible:

- Cardboard boxes. Any size, any shape, they have a powerful pull over cats. 'If it fits, I sits'.
- Stimulate your cat's senses by ensuring they have a place to sit with a clear view out of a window. They love watching what's going on, plotting the dramatic downfall of the fat pigeon on the fence from the comfort of their own home. Putting a bird or squirrel feeder in easy view of the window ups the activity level.

- Attach a grooming brush to the leg of a chair or table within easy reach of your cat. Perfect for stimulating self-grooming!

- Is every surface in your home cluttered with objects? Clear some of them away and give your cat plenty of space to jump and leap. Making your home 'multi-dimensional' will keep their brains busy; this includes giving them plenty of nooks and crannies to hide in and explore.

- Any hunting-style play is brilliant for your cat's brain. Leave plenty of objects around that your cat can easily move about and chase – balls and the ubiquitous cardboard toilet roll are perfect for this.

- If you don't mind the potential for a little bit of mess, pop two ping pong balls in a bowl of water. Your cat will love batting them around and using their brain to figure out where the balls are going to pop up next.

- Cut holes in the top of a box or other container (beware of leaving sharp edges though) and put some toys or treats inside. Your cat will need to call on their best problem-solving skills to extract the contents.

Are cats smarter than dogs?

Cats and dogs – forever pitted against each other in a battle for supremacy. Cat lovers will of course fly the flag for their beloved felines. Dog lovers will guffaw and point out how well-trained their dog is, how it responds to multiple commands, how it genuinely loves them, etc, etc. So, what's the answer? Clever kitties or smart canines?

	Cats	Dogs
Brain neurons	250 million	530 million
Hunting prowess	Excellent	Mediocre
Obeying orders	Can't be bothered	Brilliant
Contribution to society	Limited	Guide dogs, police dogs, rescue dogs, service dogs...
Size of brain (% of total body mass)	0.9%	1.2%
Brain growth	Has stayed the same for 8,000 years	Continually growing
Social skills	Non-existent unless they want something	Awesome. Sometimes too awesome
Problem solving	Persevere until they succeed	Ask humans for help
Vocabulary (average number of words)	25-35	165
Short-term memory	16 hours	5 minutes

Inconclusive, right? And so the argument will rage on for years to come.

We need to stop pitting cats and dogs against each other as each is intelligent in their own way. Every pet is an individual and we all have anecdotal evidence as to why our cat is smarter than a dog, and vice versa. The safest outcome would be to stop fussing about it and simply declare this contest a draw. Just don't tell Tiddles or Rover...

Older cats

The first weeks and months of your cat's life are an incredible learning curve. Even in adulthood, your cat is constantly learning from its environment and from you. But what happens to your cat's brain as it gets older? There does come a point when you must accept the limitations that old age brings both physically and mentally (and that goes for you as well as your cat!).

It's important that you don't stop trying to stimulate your cat's brain as they become older. They have less patience and tire more quickly, but every little bit helps. In fact, make it a priority as you may be able to slow down some of the effects old age has on their brain. Playing is still crucial so adapt games to suit any physical limitations your cat has (for example, if achy joints mean they find jumping more difficult). Regardless of their age, cats will still succumb to boredom (and potentially depression) if you don't provide the stimulation they need.

Healthy eating

Just like with humans, healthy eating plays a huge role in keeping your elderly cat's mind and body healthy. Eating well will ensure your cat's brain stays in tip top condition and can help stave off any deterioration of their faculties. For more information on beneficial foods, see Healthy Cat, Clever Cat on page 39.

Feline Cognitive Dysfunction Syndrome

Often referred to as 'cat dementia', this syndrome is very similar to Alzheimer's disease in humans. Sadly, it can lead to depression, loss of appetite, confusion, memory loss and anti-social behaviour. The onset of the syndrome can be a slow process and the symptoms are usually seen when cats are 10 years or older. If you think your cat is becoming unwell, a visit to your vet is needed and they can provide lots of helpful advice.

Although it won't cure your cat, a stimulating environment will help slow their cognitive decline. Exercise, play and training are all part of this. Healthy eating (see above) is also vital so ramp up the omega-3 and antioxidants in their diet.

PAWS FOR THOUGHT

Cats start to enter their 'senior' years when they are eight to ten years old. The signs of ageing set in when cells start to deteriorate faster than they can repair themselves.

Cats will outsmart dogs every time.

JOHN GROGAN

The lighter side of genius

Top cats

Many cats have become world famous for amazing displays of feline ingenuity. Not that you should necessarily use them as benchmarks to determine how clever your cat is. That would be like comparing yourself to Marie Curie or Albert Einstein – unrealistic and somewhat depressing. But just imagine if... just if... your cat was like one of the heroes below. Imagine the social media hits, calls from news channels, endless fortunes...

Blue the cool Californian cat

Blue made his name by being a super smart feline. According to his owner, Blue can tell the time. He gets up for breakfast at precisely the same time each day, and then at 6p.m., like clockwork, Blue heads to his bowl to wait for dinner. Blue can also take the wooden security stick from his owner's sliding glass door and push the door open to let himself out.

Clever cat or just well-trained? It's hard to tell whether Blue is extraordinary or just an ordinary moggy with a reliable internal clock who's got the hang of a few tricks. Either way, Blue is a fine example of what a cat can achieve when they set their mind to it.

Stubbs the mayor

In 1998, Stubbs the cat was elected honorary mayor of a small Alaskan town by voters who'd had enough of human candidates. This stately cat held the position until his death in 2017. He was praised for his honesty and for not raising taxes! He became quite a tourist attraction and attracted 30-40 visitors a day. Whatever next? A cat for US president? Now there's an idea...

Catmando the politician

Now for another cat with aspirations for political office... Catmando served as joint leader of the United Kingdom's Official Monster Raving Loony Party from 1999 to 2002, along with his owner, Howling Laud Hope. He's the only cat ever to have been leader of a political party. As joint leader, Catmando was part of the greatest electoral performance the party had ever seen, putting forward 15 candidates in the UK's 2001 general election.

Orangey the actor

This chic ginger tabby was best known for his role as 'Cat', the nameless companion of Audrey Hepburn in Breakfast at Tiffany's. He won numerous awards for his work during the 1950s and 60s. But it seems that Orangey was also a typical movie diva. He was described by one studio executive as "The world's meanest cat" because of his tendency to bite and scratch actors. His handler would sometimes post guard dogs at the studio entrance to stop Orangey from running away and halting production.

Scarlett the super mum

Scarlett was a stray cat living in New York when the abandoned garage she was living in caught fire. This brave mum removed all her kittens from the burning garage, one by one, risking her own life every time she went back in. Amazingly, all but one of her kittens survived their ordeal. Scarlett suffered severe burns to her eyes and ears. The happy ending to this cat 'tail' is that Scarlett and her kittens were adopted and went on to live happy lives. What a cat!

Doctor Tom

When Tom began constantly tapping the back of his owner's neck and meowing, his owner was starting to get annoyed. Yet Tom didn't stop and his owner eventually went to the doctor to get her neck looked at. The doctors discovered a cancerous lump under the skin. Tom seemed to know that his work was done – as soon as his owner had visited the doctor, he stopped pestering her. Thankfully, Tom's owner made a full recovery. For more about cats' amazing 'sixth sense', see page 51.

Dr Leon Advogato the lawyer

When people started complaining about a stray cat at the Order of Attorneys of Brazil (OAB), staff there took a stand – they hired the cat as a lawyer. Naming him Dr Leon Advogato, the learned cat later inspired the OAB's plans to launch the Instituto Dr Leon, an animal rights organisation for helping abused and abandoned animals.

Masha the lifesaver

Masha was a cat living as a communal pet amongst the residents of a Russian apartment block. One cold January, a resident came across Masha tucked up as usual in the box she slept in. However, Masha was meowing and didn't get up to greet the woman as normal. The woman was amazed to find an abandoned baby boy in the box with Masha. Without Masha keeping him warm it's extremely unlikely that the baby would have survived.

A paws for some fun...

Keeping your cat's brilliant brain stimulated can be exhausting. Time to grab a hot drink and find a comfy chair and enjoy something more light-hearted. Be prepared to groan though.

Why do clever cats always get their own way?

Because they're very purr-suasive.

Why don't cats like online shopping?

They prefer a cat-alogue.

How do we know that Earth definitely isn't flat?

Because if it was, cats would have pushed every little thing off its surface.

When you get home from work, your dog will be extremely happy to see you and will lick your face.

The cat will still be mad at you for leaving in the first place.

What's the difference between a cat and a comma?

One has claws at the end of its paws, while the other is a pause at the end of a clause.

What kind of sports car does a cat drive?

A Furrari.

What do you call a cat who just ate a duck?

A duck-filled catty puss.

Did you hear about the cat who drank 5 bowls of water?

He set a new lap record.

What is a cat's favourite magazine?

Good Mousekeeping.

Why did the judge dismiss the entire jury made up of cats?

Because each of them was guilty of purrjury.

Have you ever seen a catfish?

No. How did he hold the rod?

What happened when the cat went to the flea circus?

He stole the whole show!

How did the cat get the first prize at the bird show?

Somebody didn't shut the champion's cage properly.

Dogs will come when called.
Cats will take a message
and get back to you.

MISSY DIZICK & MARY BLY

Ten signs your cat is an evil genius

Worshipped by the Egyptians, fond of witches, loved by villains – what is it with cats? Are they our friends or are they more in touch with the dark side? Can you be sure your cat isn't plotting world domination from your living room?

1. How many times has your cat sat on your laptop keyboard and prevented you from doing anything? Do they harass you when you're trying to make a phone call? Under the pretence of wanting attention, they're trying to sever your contact with the outside world. No one can hear you scream...

2. Do cats poop in their own garden? No.

3. All those little 'accidents' you have when your cat runs through your legs or stretches out across a stair. Accidental or planned?
4. Manipulation. Your cat's cries for food or attention share a similar frequency to a baby's cry. They know how to get exactly what they want from you.
5. False affection. Do you think that your cat is rubbing around your legs because they love you? Think again. They're marking you with their scent. They own you.
6. Primed killing machines. One moment your cat is chilling on your lap purring, the next they've sprung into action to annihilate a passing spider.
7. An orchestrated national obsession. Cat videos, cat memes, cat merchandise – do you think cats really want to be laughed at on the internet? No. It's an attempt to dumb down the human race so that they can overrun us more easily.
8. They can destroy anything – gently and surreptitiously – with a simple swipe of their paw. Objects on tables and shelves aren't safe.
9. The stare. THE STARE! Has it ever felt like someone is watching you and you turn to discover it's your cat? Those eyes could penetrate a nuclear bunker.
10. Diversion tactics. Have you ever heard a crash coming from another room, followed by the sound of paws heading in another direction? One of the oldest tricks in the book and cats are brilliant at it.

Test your knowledge!

Okay, so you have an extraordinarily clever cat. But how about you? Can you live up to your cat's (very, very, very) high expectations? Time to test whether you've been paying attention. We can't promise you a kibble treat, but we've helped by making the test multiple choice. Answers at the end of the quiz. No peeking please.

1. **Your cat has the same problem-solving skills as a:**

   (a) 2–3-year-old child

   (b) 3–4-year-old child

   (c) 4–5-year-old child.

2. **How many smell receptors does your cat have in its nose?**

   (a) 150 million

   (b) 200 million

   (c) 50 million.

3. **Which of these is the brainiest breed of cat?**

   (a) Siamese

   (b) Persian

   (c) Norwegian Forest.

4. **How similar is a cat's brain to a human brain?**

   (a) 80%

   (b) 90%

   (c) 70%.

5. **How many muscles does a cat have in each ear?**

   (a) 20

   (b) 30

   (c) 40

6. **Which of these is a sign that your cat is feeling focused?**

   (a) Wide eyes and narrow pupils

   (b) Eats more food

   (c) Puffed up fur.

7. **What was Salvador Dali's ocelot called?**

   (a) Babou

   (b) Choupette

   (c) Mimi.

8. **Your cat is considered to be 'senior' at what age?**

   (a) 5–7 years

   (b) 8–10 years

   (c) 11–13 years.

9. **A cat's short-term memory is approximately...**

   (a) 10 hours

   (b) 16 hours

   (c) 20 hours.

10. **Catmando was the first cat to do what?**

   (a) Be crowned a king

   (b) Swim the English Channel

   (c) Lead a political party.

Answers

1. (a), 2. (b), 3. (a), 4. (b), 5. (b), 6. (a), 7. (a), 8. (b), 9. (b), 10. (c).

Genius training notes

Use the space below to make a note of any observations you've made about your cat's super brain power! Most of all, have fun!